Toronto Travel Guide

Attractions, Eating, Drinking, Shopping & Places To Stay

Stacey Hilton

Copyright © 2014, Astute Press
All Rights Reserved.

No part of this publication may be reproduced, stored in a retrieval system, or transmitted, in any form or by any means without the prior written permission of the publisher, nor be otherwise circulated in any form of binding or cover other than that in which it is published and without similar condition being imposed on the subsequent purchaser.

If there are any errors or omissions in copyright acknowledgements the publisher will be pleased to insert the appropriate acknowledgement in any subsequent printing of this publication.

Although we have taken all reasonable care in researching this book we make no warranty about the accuracy or completeness of its content and disclaim all liability arising from its use

Table of Contents

Toronto 7
    Culture 8
    Location & Orientation 9
    Climate & When to Visit 11

Sightseeing Highlights 13
    CN Tower 14
    Casa Loma 15
    Hockey Hall of Fame 16
    Yonge-Dundas Square 17
    Nathan Phillips Square 18
    Air Canada Centre 18
    Roger's Centre 19
    Fort York 20
    Royal Ontario Museum 21
    Ontario Science Centre 22
    Art Gallery 23
    Museum of Contemporary Canadian Art 23
    Toronto Islands 24
    Canada's Wonderland 25
    Toronto Zoo 26
    Ontario Place 27

Recommendations for the Budget Traveler 29
    Places to Stay 29
        Alexandra Hotel 29
        Ramada Plaza Downtown Toronto 30
        Glen Grove Suites & Condominiums–The Maple Leaf 30
        Knights Inn 31
    Places to Eat & Drink 32
        Grand Electric 32
        Five Guys Burgers & Fries 33
        GUU Japanese Restaurant 34
        Sneaky Dee's 34
        Nazareth Ethiopian Restaurant 35
        Church Aperitivo Bar 36
    Places to Shop 36

Eaton Centre..36
Kensington Market...37
St. Lawrence Market..38
Yonge Street..39

Montreal..41
Culture..43
Location & Orientation..44
Climate & When to Visit..46

Sightseeing Highlights...47
Old Montreal..47
Place d'Armes...48
Montreal History Center...49
Granite Obelisk..49
Notre-Dame Basilica..50
Parc du Mont-Royal..50
Olympic Park..51
La Ronde Amusement Park..52
Botanical Gardens..53
Alpine Garden..53
First Nation's Garden..53
Japanese Garden..54
Chinese Garden..54
St. Joseph's Oratory...55
Montreal's Underground City....................................56
Jean Talon Market..57
Museum of Archeology & History............................57
Museum of Fine Arts...58
Museum of Contemporary Arts.................................59
Science Center..59
Quebec City..60
Getting There...62
Getting Around...62
When to Go..63
What to See..64

Recommendations for the Budget Traveler.........67
Places to Stay...67
Celebrities Hotel...67
Hotel de Paris Montreal...68
Auberge Montreal Youth Hostel.............................69
HI-Montreal Youth Hostel...69

Auberge De Jeunesse Alexandrie 70
Places to Eat & Drink **70**
   Espace Cafe & Espresso Bar 70
   Schwartz's 71
   La Banquise 71
   Stash Café 72
   Vices et Versa 73
Places to Shop **74**
   Jeans, Jeans, Jeans 74
   Harmonie Gifts & Souvenirs 74
   Mountain Equipment Co-Op 75
   Friperie Saint-Laurent 75
   Chabanel Warehouses 76

TORONTO & MONTREAL TRAVEL GUIDE

Toronto

Toronto is the largest city in Canada and the capital city of the province of Ontario. Known as the New York of Canada, Toronto is a hotbed for culture, art and entertainment. Like its American counterpart, Toronto offers a fast-paced, bustling lifestyle which the visitor will find mesmerizing.

With a population of roughly 3 million, the city is part of a zone called the Greater Toronto Area, or GTA for short, which itself is home to over 6 million people.

The city has gained popularity the world over in recent years as one of the most culturally and ethnically diverse cities on the planet, and rightfully so. Toronto is not a melting pot; rather, it is a majestic mosaic of cultures from all over the globe, where each puzzle piece fits perfectly alongside the others.

You can expect anything and everything from a city like Toronto. There are music festivals, good beaches, parks, sports venues, museums and a myriad of restaurants, bars and nightclubs to choose from. Whether you're staying for a just few days or a year, there is never enough time to fully experience all that Toronto has to offer, so soak up as much of the excitement as you can while you're here.

Culture

Statistically speaking, Toronto (pronounced "Tuh-ron-no" by Canadians) is second only to Miami for having the highest percentage of foreign-born residents, with more than half of its residents being born outside of the country. However, while Miami's immigrant population consists primarily of Cubans and Latin Americans, that of Toronto represents over 80 ethnicities, with no single predominant culture.

This multiculturalism is reflected in the city's many festivals, concerts, museums, shops, markets, restaurants, ethnic neighbourhoods, and public services. Ambling around, you will notice the multilingual street signs. You may come across a Caribbean Carnival, a film festival, or a Shakespeare production in High Park.

You may pass through Chinatown, Kensington Market, Greek Town, Korea Town, Roncesvalle, Corso Italia, Little Italy, Little India and Little Jamaica and Little Portugal, among other neighborhoods.

Likewise, many public services boast their ability to provide services in several languages. Most banks can service Torontonians in English as well as varieties of Chinese and Italian or other languages prevalent in the area. If you run into trouble, Toronto's 9-1-1 emergency services are prepared to respond in over 150 different languages.

Location & Orientation

Toronto is located at the heart of the GTA, or Greater Toronto Area, and is part of a larger region known as the Golden Horseshoe, which stretches around Lake Ontario and also touches parts of Lake Erie and Georgian Bay. The city can be divided into 6 zones or boroughs: Old Toronto (which includes Downtown, the West End, the East End, Midtown and the Islands), Etobicoke (pronounced "A-toe-bi-koe"), York, East York, North York and Scarborough.

Servicing the GTA are 3 airports, the chief of which is Toronto Pearson International Airport, 30-50 minutes from the downtown core. There is also Billy Bishop Toronto City Centre Airport, more commonly known as "The Island Airport", which handles regional flights only, and Hamilton International Airport. Budget travelers may also want to look into flights to and from Buffalo-Niagara International Airport. Though it is across the border, Megabus runs from downtown Toronto to the airport, and flights tend to be cheaper, so it is a viable option.

There are several options you may want to consider for getting around Toronto. The city is very large, but traffic can be heavy during rush-hour, and taxis and parking fees expensive, so the frugal traveler should consider public transportation. The subway system is straightforward, quick and efficient, though with only 4 lines it may not meet all your needs. Thankfully, there is also a bus system, streetcar system, quasi-subway line and regional train, and bus system called GO Transit. The buses, streetcars and subway are all part of the TTC (Toronto Transit Commission). Single fares are usually $2.50-$3.00, though express and lengthier trips will cost more. Depending on the length of your visit and how often you plan to be using public transportation, you may want to consider a daily ($10.50) or weekly ($37.50) TTC pass. Weekly GTA passes are $54.

Climate & When to Visit

Toronto does not suffer very harsh winters like the rest of the country, thanks to its location in the South near the American border. You can expect high temperatures in the wintertime to hover around freezing (0° Celsius or 32° Fahrenheit), and nightly lows of around -5 degrees Celsius (23°F). There are, however, bouts of colder weather coming in from the North, and snowstorms mixed with ice and rain are not uncommon, often disrupting traffic and other travel schedules. Consistent with the rest of the country, the coldest month is January but snowfall can occur anytime from November to mid-April, so come prepared with warm clothing and waterproof boots or shoes. Though cold and sometimes dreary, the winter can be enchanting and seem to cast some sort of spell with its crisp blankets of snow.

On the contrast, the summer months can get quite hot and humid. Daily highs average out at around 27 degrees Celsius (80°F), not including humidity, and nightly lows around 18 (65°F). Hotter days, peaking in the mid-30s, are becoming more and more common.

August and September are the wettest months due to thunderstorms, but the springtime brings a considerable amount of rain as well. Though Toronto's vibrancy extends even through the winter, late spring/early summer and early fall are considered to be the best times to visit. During this time, the temperatures are comfortable and the crowds are small, with the peak tourist season being mid-summer.

Toronto has something to offer in every season, with attractions and events year-round. Whenever you decide to come, there's sure to be more than a few things to enjoy.

Sightseeing Highlights

Depending on how long you will be in Toronto, and how many sights you want to see, you may want to consider getting the Toronto CityPASS. This gives you 43% off select attractions, and allows you to skip most lines. The pass costs a total of $69.50 and grants access to the CN Tower, Toronto Zoo, Casa Loma, Ontario Science Centre and the Royal Ontario Museum. Purchase your pass at the zoo's box office or online at www.citypass.com.

CN Tower

www.cntower.ca
301 Front Street West, Toronto, Ontario M5V 2T6
(416) 868-6937

Classified in 1995 as one of the Seven Wonders of the Modern World, the CN Tower is the icon which defines Toronto's skyline. It was originally built in 1976 in order to respond to existing transmission towers problems in the city. Today, towering at over 553 meters (over 1,815 ft.), it is Toronto's centre of telecommunications, serves over 16 Canadian television and FM radio stations, and, as the tallest free-standing structure in the Western hemisphere, is an internationally renowned architectural symbol.

At 346 meters (1,136 ft.), the LookOut Level offers an astonishing view of the city. If you're not satisfied, though, the SkyPod level offers a 360° perspective at 447m (1,465 ft.) high overlooking the city, Lake Ontario and beyond.

For a discounted price, buy your tickets online. Tickets for the LookOut Level are $27.50 for adults, and the SkyPod level will cost you an additional $12.00. The CN Tower is open every day of the year, with the exception of Christmas Day, from 9 a.m. to 10 p.m. though hours may change seasonally.

For the more daring individuals, an EdgeWalk experience has recently been introduced. For the hefty price of $175.00, you can walk outside around the roof's circumference (while harnessed) and literally get a bird's eye view of the city, not to mention a wicked photo. Another feature for the high-roller is 360, the revolving restaurant near the top of the tower. 360 is the epitome of extravagance. With the purchase of a main course, access to the LookOut and Glass Floor is included. For both these experiences, make sure you book a reservation well in advance.

Casa Loma

http://casaloma.org/
1 Austin Terrace, Toronto, Ontario M5R 1X8
(416) 923-1171

Located in midtown, Casa Loma is Toronto's castle. Though construction was halted in 1914 due to the start of World War I, Sir Henry Pellatt purchased the land and commissioned construction in 1911 for the largest private residence in Canada, with a total of 98 rooms.

Architect E.J. Lennox, was responsible for the design of the mansion, as well as several other landmarks around the city. In 1933, the city seized Casa Loma for over $27,000 in back taxes, and in 1937 it was opened as a museum. Today, it is undergoing an exterior restoration.

Casa Loma is open daily from 9:30 a.m. to 5:00 p.m., and is closed only on Christmas day. General admission for adults is $20.55.

Hockey Hall of Fame

http://www.hhof.com/
Brookfield Place, 30 Yonge Street, Toronto, Ontario M5E 1X8
(416) 360-7765

It is difficult to describe the love that Canada has for hockey. It is much more than the pastime that gets Canadians through unforgiving winters; it is a pinnacle of national pride and identity. So it was only natural that, following the opening of several other halls of fame, Captain James Sutherland started a motion that hockey should have its own to call home.

Having argued that Kingston, Ontario was the birthplace of hockey, Sutherland convinced the NHL and CAHA (Canadian Amateur Hockey Association) to agree to establish a Hockey Hall of Fame in that city. The first members were inducted while plans were made and construction began. However, construction proved to be very costly, and after much delay, the NHL withdrew its support and decided to relocate the Hall of Fame in Toronto.

Today, General admission will run you $17.50, and true hockey fans will be glad to know that they can get their picture taken with the Stanley Cup for an additional $5.00 if the ticket is booked online.

Yonge-Dundas Square

http://www.ydsquare.ca/

Yonge-Dundas Square (commonly referred to as "Dundas Square" by locals) is a focal point for the downtown community of Toronto. Aptly named, it is at the corner of Yonge Street, which was formerly the longest street in the world, and Dundas Street, and is an open public space that can also be used as a venue to accommodate some of the city's events. Most of these events are free, including concerts, receptions, films, theatrical events, and other promotions and celebrations.

The square came about after the city of Toronto launched a competition in 1998 for the design of a new square in order to reintroduce some of the old vitality into Yonge Street. Today, it offers an exciting yet serene scene at the heart of the city to sit and people-watch amidst the sometimes crazy downtown core. The square offers free Wi-Fi internet as well, and since it is public, it never closes.

Nathan Phillips Square

If Toronto is the New York of Canada, Nathan Phillips square is equivalent of the Times Square of Toronto. On New Year's Eve, you can watch the ball drop here alongside thousands of other people. Named after Nathan Phillips, who was the Mayor of Toronto from 1955 to 1962, it is located immediately in front of City Hall on the corner of Queen and Bay Streets, just a few blocks from Dundas Square.

Like Dundas Square, it is the host of many of the city's special events. One of the world's largest underground parking garages is located directly beneath the square, holding up to 2,400 cars. The square also showcases several sculptures and landmarks: the Freedom Arches, the Peace Garden, a statue of Sir Winston Churchill, and the reflecting pool which, in winter, is transformed into a public skating rink. A Speaker's Corner podium was also installed at the south west corner in an effort to promote free speech in Toronto. Anyone who wishes may express their opinions on camera, though, sadly, the recordings are no longer televised.

Air Canada Centre

http://www.theaircanadacentre.com/

If you want an authentic Canadian experience, an NHL hockey game doesn't leave much to be desired.

Oddly enough, the NHL's Toronto Maple Leafs call the Air Canada Centre their home, and not the Maple Leaf Gardens. The Air Canada Centre is one of the country's leading venues for sports and entertainment, and has hosted over 2,000 events. Various other sports teams play at the centre as well, including the Toronto Raptors and the Toronto Rock Lacrosse Team. However, tickets can be steep, especially during the playoffs.

Roger's Centre

http://www.rogerscentre.com/
One Blue Jays Way, Toronto, Ontario M5V 1J3
416-341-1000 or 1-855-985-5000

If you're traveling on a budget but would still like to experience a live sports event in Toronto, a Blue Jays baseball game is your best option. Conveniently located downtown, next to the CN Tower, you can see a game at the Roger's Centre, formerly known as the SkyDome, for as little as $10.00. Different combination tickets are available online, such as the Grand Slam Combo for $39.00 which includes your ticket, food and beverages.

Fort York

http://www.fortyork.ca/
250 Fort York Boulevard, Toronto, ON M5V 3K9
416-392-6907

Over 200 years ago, the huge city of Toronto was but a small community. Lieutenant Governor John Graves Simcoe, wary of the building tension between the British and Americans, ordered construction of a stronghold in 1793 in order to defend and control Lake Ontario. The provincial capital of Upper Canada was moved from Niagara Falls to Toronto, Toronto was renamed 'York', and a civilian settlement soon followed. A Government House was built as well as parliament buildings and a garrison east of modern day Bathurst Street. Simcoe's successor, Major-General Isaac Brock, strengthened the fort in 1811 in anticipation of conflicts.

In 1812, the Americans declared war and invaded Canada, and on April 27th, 1813, York was attacked. Several of the original buildings were burned or destroyed, but the British prevailed and rebuilt. Many of the buildings that you see today were built immediately after the war.

Today, Fort York's buildings are among the oldest in Toronto, and its walls surround the largest collection of original buildings from the War of 1812. The fort is operated as a museum, and is open 361 days a year. Admission for adults is $9.00, but the hours of operation vary, so make sure to check online when planning your visit.

Royal Ontario Museum

http://www.rom.on.ca/en
100 Queen's Park, Toronto, ON M5S 2C6
416.586.8000

By far, the most unique and unconventional museum in Toronto is the ROM. It is the country's largest museum of world culture and natural history. With a convenient downtown location, it attracts over one million visitors every year. The ROM boasts over 40 galleries, ranging in theme from fossils, to African art, to Canadian history, to clothing and interior design. It also features a crystalline-formed and originally controversial new entrance, "The Crystal".

The ROM's most eccentric feature, however, is its "Friday Night Live". Throughout May and June, the museum turns discotheque on Fridays after 7 p.m., and visitors can enjoy beverages and live music amongst dinosaurs and prestigious paintings. Tickets for these events are $12 and should be bought in advance on the museum's website.

Ontario Science Centre

http://www.ontariosciencecentre.ca
770 Don Mills Road, Toronto, ON M3C 1T3
416-696-1000

When it first opened in 1969, the Ontario Science Centre was a pioneer for its unique hands-on approach to science. The centre differs from conventional museums in that the exhibits are not for display only; rather, they are mostly interactive. The exhibits feature just about every theme that can be found in science and in nature, ranging from anatomy to music, and from geology to astronomy, with some miscellaneous exhibits. Such exhibits have included "Happy Potter The Exhibition" and "Body Worlds", and the latest "Game On 2.0", an exhibition on the history of video games. The centre also has its own school, which offers credited University Preparation courses in various science subjects, and an IMAX theatre.

The Ontario Science Centre is open 7 days a week, 364 days a year (the exception being Christmas Day). Hours are 10 a.m. to 4 p.m. Monday to Friday, and 10 a.m. to 5 p.m. on weekends and holidays. General admission is $22.00 for adults.

Art Gallery

http://www.ago.net
317 Dundas Street West, Toronto, Ontario, M5T 1G4
1-877-225-4246 or 416-979-6648

This gorgeous, modern building is located in the downtown Grange Park district, and features the largest existing collection of Canadian art. It also showcases a considerable number of works from Europe, Africa and Oceania, and works from the Renaissance and Baroque eras. In addition to these galleries, the AGO also holds many sculptures, an extensive library, a gallery workshop space, a restaurant, research centre and lecture hall, among other features. It is open from 10 a.m. to 5:30 p.m. daily, but closed on Mondays. General admission is normally $19.50 for adults, but free on Wednesday nights from 6-8:30 p.m.

Museum of Contemporary Canadian Art

www.mocca.ca
952 Queen Street West, Toronto, Ontario M6J 1G8
(416) 395-0067

The MOCCA features two large exhibition spaces dedicated to Canadian and international artists who address challenging topical issues.

The works showcased in this museum are always innovative and influential. Definitely worth a look, hours are Tuesday to Sunday, 11 a.m. to 6 p.m., and admission is a refreshing 'pay what you can'.

Toronto Islands

http://torontoislands.org/

The Toronto Islands are a tranquil haven amongst a huge, bustling metropolis. They are made up of a chain of a dozen small islands, the largest of which are Toronto Island (or Centre Island), Middle Island, Ward's Island, Olympic Island and Algonquin Island. They are home to a small residential community, making them the largest urban car-free community in North America.

To reach the islands, you can take a ferry from the Ferrydocks at 9 Queen's Quay West, located south of Queen's Quay between Yonge and Bay Streets.

The ferry costs $7.00, including return, can accommodate recreational bicycles, and leaves approximately every 30 minutes on weekends and holidays (less often during the week). You can take a ferry either to Ward's Island, Centre Island or Hanlan's point. Whichever direction you choose to take, the ride lasts about 15 minutes each way. Water taxis are also available, but for a higher price. For more information on schedules, go to http://www.toronto.ca/parks/island/ferry-schedule.htm.

Once you arrive at your destination on any of the islands, you can rent a canoe, bicycle or quadracycle, play some disc golf, volleyball, tennis or softball, have a barbeque on one of the fire pits in the picnic areas, or simply just lie on the beach soaking up the sun and admiring the city skyline from a distance. If you happen to be in Toronto on a particularly beautiful day, it is a great way to escape the stresses of the city and just relax for the day.

Canada's Wonderland

https://www.canadaswonderland.com/
9580 Jane Street, Vaughan, ON L6A 1S6
(905) 832-8131

Canada's Wonderland, previously known as Paramount Canada's Wonderland, is the country's first and largest major theme park. One of the park's attractions is International Street, similar to the Walt Disney Parks' Main Street, U.S.A, with Latin, Scandinavian, Mediterranean and Alpine themed buildings.

In earlier years, the stores in this area sold high-quality imported goods in accordance with their themed buildings, and restaurants sold unconventional foods, also themed, such as shrimp, paella and smoked sausage.

The park also features a 20 acre waterpark, Splash Works, a Medieval Faire, Action Zone, Happyland of Hanna-Barbera area, Kidzville, Zoom Zone, and Planet Snoopy.

With a total of 68 rides including 16 roller coasters, and 11 water rides, Canada's Wonderland attracts over 3 million visitors per year. The most recent and renowned rides are Leviathan and Behemoth. At over 93 meters (306 feet), Leviathan is the tallest ride in the park and lasts almost three and a half minutes. Riders are dropped from the peak at an 80 degree angle, reaching speeds of 148 km/hr. Behemoth is known for its 180 degree hairpin turn and 2 helixes.

Tickets are $39.99 for adults when purchased online. With all its thrills and attractions, there's sure to be something for everyone at Canada's Wonderland.

Toronto Zoo

http://torontozoo.com
2000 Meadowvale Rd, Toronto, ON M1B 5K7
416-392-5929

The Toronto Zoo is one of the largest zoos in the world at 710 acres, and with over 10km of walking trails.

It is located near the Rouge River in Scarborough, about 30 minutes from downtown, and is accessible by public transit.

The zoo is home to over 5,000 animals representing over 500 species, which are divided into seven zoogeographic regions: Indo-Malaya, Africa, the Americas, Australasia, Eurasia, Canadian Domain and the Tundra Trek.

Highlights include a 5-acre Polar Bear habitat, a Gorilla Rainforest, and the Great Barrier Reef. There is also a special Discovery Zone, which features an interactive experience for children called the Kids Zoo, a two-acre water park called Splash Island, and the Waterside Theatre. General admission for adults is $28.00.

Ontario Place

http://www.ontarioplace.com/
955 Lake Shore Blvd W, Toronto, ON M6K 3B9
(416) 314-9900

Currently undergoing revitalization, Ontario Place is a multi-purpose site located on the shore of Lake Ontario, just south of Exhibition Place. It was opened over 40 years ago as a theme park of the same name which closed in 2011. It consists of three artificially constructed and landscaped islands.

Today, the Ontario Place Marino is still open, as well as The Molson Canadian Ampitheatre, Echo Beach, and Atlantis Pavilion.

TORONTO & MONTREAL TRAVEL GUIDE

Recommendations for the Budget Traveler

Places to Stay

Alexandra Hotel

http://alexandrahotel.com/
77 Ryerson Avenue, Toronto, Ontario M5T 2V4
(416) 504-2121

Specifically seeking to accommodate budget travelers who value convenience, the Alexandra Hotel is located at the heart of downtown Toronto, near the Kensington Market, Chinatown, Little Italy and the University of Toronto. Streetcars and subway stops are also within walking distance.

Each room comes equipped with one double bed and one twin bed, a private bath with full tub, a kitchenette, cable TV, internet and an individually controlled air conditioner and heater. The best feature of this hotel is that, with an average of $99.95 per night, its price is hard to beat.

Ramada Plaza Downtown Toronto

http://www.ramadaplazatoronto.com/
300 Jarvis Street, Toronto, ON M5B 2C5
1-855-247-4371

You can't get any closer to downtown than this. At 2 blocks from Yonge Street, a quarter-mile from the Eaton Centre, this high-rise is located in Toronto's Garden District, home to the city's Gay Village, Allan Gardens and several heritage buildings. If you happen to be visiting Toronto during its world-famous Pride celebrations, this is where you want to stay.

Amenities include a business center, indoor pool, spa tub, sauna, fitness facilities, and an on-site restaurant. All guestrooms have complimentary wireless Internet access, phones, cable TV, climate control and coffeemakers.

Glen Grove Suites & Condominiums-- The Maple Leaf

http://www.glengrove.com/downtown/maple_leaf.htm
390 Queens Quay W Toronto, ON - M5V 3T1
416-489-8441 or 1-800-565-3024

At the heart of downtown Toronto, this beautiful condominium residence is within walking distance from the CN Tower, Skydome, and most other of the city's landmarks.

You are literally just steps away from the harbourfront, ferry docks and lake, parks, subways, theatres, restaurants and countless other attractions.

You can stay for a minimum of 3 nights at The Maple Leaf Quay, a state-of-the-art building complete with hot tub and sauna, fitness centre, billiards table and media room, meeting room, an indoor golf driving range, and rooftop seating with barbeque. Each room features a full kitchen with microwave and dishwasher, high-speed Wi-Fi, TV/DVD entertainment centre, complimentary Starter Pack which includes coffee, tea bags and other essentials, and a private phone with free local calls.

When you stay with Glen Grove, you really do have all the comforts of home for the price of an affordable hotel. Daily rates vary from $109-199, depending on time of the year and number of rooms you desire.

Knights Inn

http://knightsinntoronto.com/
117 Pembroke St, Toronto, ON, M5A2N9
1-866-299-2910

Knights Inn Toronto hotel is located right downtown, steps away from the Allan Gardens, and within walking distance to the Eaton Centre, Dundas Square, and many, many more attractions. The history property has been around since the York period, though its rooms have been newly renovated.

Its amenities feature free internet access, a microwave and fridge in the breakfast area, luggage storage, and best of all, complimentary continental breakfast. The entire property is smoke-free. Accommodation starts at the low price of $79.

Places to Eat & Drink

Grand Electric

http://www.grandelectricbar.com/
1330 Queen Street West, Parkdale, M6K1L4
416.627.3459

Located in Parkdale, west of downtown, this taco restaurant is famous for its fish tacos and bourbon selection. It is extremely informal, serves deliciously juicy and authentic food, and is unexpectedly cheap. They don't take reservations and they tell it like it is, which is part of the appeal. This place is open for lunch every day, and open for dinner from 5:30 p.m. until midnight or later. The vibe is a mix of relaxed and hearty, with some hip hop playing in the background and the sounds of loud laughter and chatter swirling about.

Though the chalkboard menu changes often, you can expect an assortment of tacos, burritos, appetizers and daily specials. If you're feelings adventurous and it's on the menu, try the beef cheek or pigs tail. Tacos are generally around $3 each, which for Toronto is very reasonable, and specials are usually around $10-$15.

Grand Electric is also revered for its drink selection; a huge assortment of bourbon, and delicious mixed drinks such as Horchada or Michelada. Though there can sometimes be a line out the door and down the block, the food and drinks at Grand Electric are certainly worth the wait.

Five Guys Burgers & Fries

http://www.fiveguys.com
329 Yonge Street, Toronto, ON M5B 1A1
416-591-0404

The Murrell brothers decided to open a burger joint in 1986 in Washington, DC. It quickly gained a following and expanded throughout the country. Today, Five Guys Burgers and Fries has several locations in Toronto, so if you happen to be outside the downtown core, take a look at their website for other locations. They use only fresh ingredients – nothing is ever frozen, only cooled – they use only peanut oil, and all menu items are trans-fat free. If you've got a hankering for some delicious comfort food, but want to be healthy, Five Guys is the way to go.

There are over 250,000 possible ways to order a burger at Five Guys, and you can take your fries plain or Cajun style. Prices are very affordable; a full meal will cost you $10-15.

GUU Japanese Restaurant

http://guu-izakaya.com/toronto/
398 Church Street Toronto, O.N. M5B 2A2
416-977-0999

Guu is a Japanese Izakaya restaurant, which is basically a bar that serves food along with its drinks. It is equipped with a full sake bar, and the food is interesting, to say the least. It is a delicious medley of authentic Japanese and contemporary taste, which somehow work harmoniously together. They are open for dinner and stay open late every day of the week.

Expect a bustling atmosphere and a friendly staff. Prices for most items are under $10.

Though the line-up can sometimes be long, the culinary experience at GUU is worth the wait.

Sneaky Dee's

http://sneaky-dees.com
431 College St., Toronto, ON M5T 1T1
(416) 603-3090

Sneaky Dee's is popular among students for its reasonable prices, lively and homey atmosphere, and connection to the music scene.

It opened its doors to the city in 1987 and hasn't looked back. Very much an integral part of Toronto's culture, it is also a concert venue which hosts a variety of different parties every week.

The food is pub and Tex-Mex style, and there is a different special every night of the week, from ribs and wings to pork sliders and fajitas. For an unforgettable nacho platter, get the King's Crown. No matter where you're from, you'll feel at home at Sneaky Dee's.

Nazareth Ethiopian Restaurant

969 Bloor Street W
Toronto, ON M6H 1L7
(416) 535-0797

Nazareth is an Ethiopian restaurant in Bloorcourt known for its delicious food, friendly staff, generous portions and low prices. Many Torontonians rave that this is the best Ethiopian food in town. There are only 8 items on the menu, but every single option will satisfy your taste buds. There is a vegetarian option which is extremely popular, even among meat-eaters.

Due to its popularity, you can expect line-ups, but platters are around $10 each and the portions are large enough to feed two. Beer is $4. At that price, it's hard to be disappointed.

Church Aperitivo Bar

http://churchaperitivobar.com/
1090 Queen Street West, Toronto ON
416 537 1090

You'd think that an Italian restaurant which offers a variety of carefully crafted cocktails, fine cuisine and a trendy atmosphere would be out of the question for the frugal traveler, but you'd be wrong. Church Aperitivo bar is very affordable, especially for its kind. Come on a Wednesday or a Friday from 5-7 p.m. or Saturday from 5-6:30 p.m. for delicious complimentary appetizers with the purchase of an equally delicious beverage.

Places to Shop

Toronto is well-known throughout Canada and beyond for its unbelievable shopping. With such incredible variety, you are sure to find whatever it is you're looking for.

Eaton Centre

http://www.torontoeatoncentre.com
220 Yonge Street, Toronto, ON, M5B 2H1
(416) 598-8560

At the heart of downtown Toronto, there is a mall which boasts over 320 shops, restaurants and other services.

The Eaton Centre is aptly named after the Eaton's department store which once anchored it. Conveniently located on the subway line ad connected to both Dundas and Queen Stations, the mall attracts over one million visitors per week, making it Toronto's number one tourist attraction.

The mall features Canada's largest store, the Hudson Bay department store, and interior passages that form part of Toronto's underground pedestrian network, PATH. It is enclosed by Yonge Street to the East, Queen Street West to the South, Dundas Street West to the North, and James Street and Trinity Square to the West. The Eaton Centre is an unexpected architectural and shopping gem not to be overlooked.

Kensington Market

www.kensington-market.ca

Kensington Market is by far the most vibrant and diverse part of Toronto. It is located just west of downtown and bordered by Spadina to the East, Dundas Street W. to the South, Bathurst Street to the West and College Street to the North. If you are already downtown, it is best to find Kensington on foot, though several street cars run through it.

The market is comprised of many shops, ethnic grocery stores, restaurants, bars, cafes and several art and entertainment venues. It has been designated a National Historic Site of Canada, and is also known for its Victorian style houses and buildings. In the early twentieth century, the area was populated mostly by eastern European Jewish immigrants and some Italians. It was one of the poorer areas of the city, and became known as the "Jewish Market", selling knickknacks and gifts reminiscent of Europe.

After the Second World War, most of the Jewish population moved North to the suburbs, which made room for a wave of new Caribbean and East Asian immigrants. Throughout the years, many refugees and other immigrants from troubled countries have made their way to the area, adding to its diversity. Additionally, Chinatown is located just East of Kensington.

Thanks to its narrow streets, Kensington is mostly a pedestrian area. You can stroll from shop to shop, discovering great finds and deals on clothing, furniture and a vast array of unique knickknacks and gifts.

St. Lawrence Market

http://www.stlawrencemarket.com/
92 - 95 Front Street East, Toronto
(416) 392-7219

The St. Lawrence Market was named the world's best food market by National Geogrpahic.

It has two different buildings: the St. Lawrence North and St. Lawrence South. The first hosts weekly farmer's markets and antique markets, and the latter hosts restaurants, a gallery, and a variety of shops, bakeries and delis. Free wireless internet is provided throughout the South Market.

The market is embedded deep in Toronto's history; it served at the city's first permanent city hall and jail house in the nineteenth century. Today, it is home to over 50 vendors of meat, cheese, fruits and vegetables on the first floor alone, The Market Gallery on the second floor, and a cooking school on the mezzanine floor. In total, there are over 120 vendors who enthusiastically display their life's passion.

Yonge Street

http://downtownyonge.com/

The construction of Yonge Street has been designated as an Event of National Historic Significance in Canada, as it was once the longest street in the world at 1,896 kilometres long (1,178 miles). It was an integral part of the planning and settlement of the city back in the 1790's. Starting at Queen's Quay and making its way through several major cities, including Vaughan and Markham, Yonge Street is often referred to as "Main Street Ontario", and was the site of Canada's first subway line.

Today, there are countless retailers, restaurants, bars and other businesses along Yonge Street. You can take in the essence of downtown Toronto while walking down the street, do some window shopping, and score some pretty exceptional deals.

Montreal

One of the liveliest and most cosmopolitan cities in Canada, Montreal in Quebec is an island situated between the Ottawa and St. Lawrence rivers. At its center is the "mountain", Mont-Royal after which the city is named.

The city itself is divided in half between the French speaking eastside and the English speaking west. With a population of 2 million in the city and 4 million around it, the city of Montreal (pronounced Mawn-ray-al in French) is home to the second largest French-speaking population outside of Paris.

One of the most livable cities in the world, Montreal compares to cities such as Vienna, Madrid and Boston with its mixture of history, culture and contemporary chic. With its European influence, Montreal can be compared to New Orleans.

The city itself can be a bit confusing. Early planners wrongly thought the St. Lawrence River ran from west to east when, in fact, runs from south to north. Standing on a street running "north" you are actually looking west.

Montreal has a reputation as a free-spirited city where a lively joie-de-vivre is the order of the day. This tradition dates back to the 1920's when it became a haven for thirsty Americans seeking liquor denied them by prohibition. With the liquor came raucous good times, music and a slight bawdiness. While the times have caught up with its freewheeling ways, Montreal continues to be a mecca for progressive culture, tolerance and a laid-back approach to life.

Today, Montreal combines 21st century sophistication with 18th century historical influence. In Old Montreal or Vieux-Montréal, architecture and cobble stone streets remain as testament to its European roots, while the city boasts fashions and trends that rival Milan and New York. Its population is a melting pot of influences derived from early settlers from Europe and the United Kingdom. Straddled between the old world and the new with its gumbo of diverse cultures, Montreal is unique.

With its rich and varied history, Montreal will appeal to those looking for culture that is little known outside its borders. As one of the world's major cities, it boasts some of the finest cultural venues on earth. Its art museums and music halls are among the best there are. Montreal is a hockey mad city. Sport's fans lucky enough to get a ticket to a Canadiens' game will see one of the NHL's finest teams playing in front of the game's most rabid fans. Young people, students and backpackers will find a wealth of things to do. In the summertime, Montreal comes alive with music festivals, arts and crafts shows and street performers. As a college town, Montreal's nightlife is buzzing with places where people can meet, mingle and dance the night away in clubs catering to every musical taste.

Culture

Originally settled by the French, and then taken over by the British before finally being absorbed into Canada, Montreal has a rich cultural background to draw from. Predominantly Francophone, it is the cultural capital of Quebec. Many events such as circuses, theater, music, television and radio shows are all done in French.

Split down the middle of Saint Laurent Boulevard and living on its west side are the Anglophones or English speakers. In years past there have been some tensions between the two cultures as the Francophone of Quebec look to make it a separate country. Visitors will not find this tension readily apparent as Montreal is one of the world's safest cities. 66% of the population is bilingual.

Montreal has a thriving music scene. On Quebec's national holiday, musicians from around the world gather for a musical festival. It is one of the stops on many major rock bands tours with some playing Olympic Stadium. The city hosts the Montreal International Jazz Festival that features all styles of jazz. Other festivals include Mutek, the electronic music festival, the Montreal Reggae Festival, the African Nights festival known as Festival International Nuits Afrique. There is a large local music scene with musicians performing primarily in French. The Montreal Symphony Orchestra and the Opéra de Montréal regularly perform.

The city is also the home of the internationally renowned Cirque de Soleil. Its primary ballet company is Les Grands Ballets Canadiens. For those with a taste for modern dance, La La La Human Steps is a troupe of international renown.

Location & Orientation

Montreal is the cultural and economic center of Quebec Province. Its political capital is in Quebec City. In central Montreal you'll find the Ville-Marie borough which consists of downtown, the old city, Parc Jean-Drapeau and the Quartier Latin-le Village. The Plateau Mont-Royal is a trendy, upscale neighborhood east of the Parc du Mont-Royal. Other districts include the trendy Outremont, Mile End, Rosemont-La-Petit-Patrie, South West, Côte-des-Neiges, and Hochelaga-Maisonneuve.

The city is only 20 miles from Pierre Elliot Trudeau Airport. Most major Canadian and American airlines fly into Montreal as well as international carriers British Airways, KLM, Lufthansa, and Swiss International Airlines.

An Amtrak train running from New York arrives in Montreal's downtown Central Station. The ten-hour ride is considered one of the world's great train trips. Running along the Hudson River, the train speeds through the scenic vistas of Upstate New York before circling the shores of Lake Champlain. The ride departs New York in the morning and arrives in Montreal in the early evening, leaving enough time for dinner and a good night's sleep.

Getting around Montreal is quite easy and very inexpensive. The quickest, most efficient way to visit the city is by its metro system. This bike friendly system takes you to all the major destinations. Montreal stations are reminiscent of those found in Stockholm and Moscow as each one has its own unique architecture and style. 2500 buses serve the entire city. To hear the next three arrivals call A-U-T-O-B-U-S (514-288-6287). Many stops have the complete route, destination and arrival and departure times listed.

Full information can be found here:
http://www.stm.info/English/Metro/a-index.htm

Climate & When to Visit

Given its northerly latitude, Montreal can be quite cold, snowy and slushy during the late autumn to early spring months. A short spring arrives in early May and lasts till mid-June. Summers can be somewhat humid. Heat waves sweep over the city in July and August, though they tend to be brief and almost always give way to pleasant temperatures by evening. Autumn lasts from mid-September to mid-October as warm to moderate temperatures give way to chilly evenings. Like the New England states, Montreal is ablaze in color as the maple trees begin to turn.

http://www.weather.com/weather/today/Montreal+CAXX0301:1:CA

Sightseeing Highlights

Old Montreal

http://www.vieux.montreal.qc.ca/eng/accueila.htm

This is the heart of Montreal, the original city. It is architecturally unique in all of North America. While the rest of the city has grown up around it, Old Montreal retains the same cobble stone streets and buildings it had soon after the city was founded. It looks as if it could be used as a backdrop for a movie set in the 19th century. Only 1.2 kilometers (0.8 of a mile) long and half as wide, the attractions of Old Montreal can easily be visited on foot.

Place d'Armes

This square gets its name from the time when Maisonneuve shot and killed an Iroquois chief. A statue of him planting the Royal Standard of France stands in the middle of the square. Each corner of the statue has a scene of significance. On one corner is Maisonneuve's lieutenant Lambert Closse with his dog Pilote. Closse died fighting the Iroquois. Kneeling on the northwest corner is Charles le Moyne. Le Moyne's sons would go on to found Louisiana. Jeanne Mance, an early settler, is depicted nursing an Amerindian child. Lastly is a depiction of an Iroquois Indian who were the original settlers of the region. On a bas relief is a depiction of Montreal's greatest hero, Dollard des Ormeaux, Maisonneuve shooting an Indian, the first mass and a depiction of the Society of Our Lady of Montreal.

The buildings around the Place d'Armes are quite interesting. Looking like a Scottish castle, the red stoned office tower (1889) was built as Montreal's first skyscraper. The Bank of Montreal (1845) is a domed building resembling the Pantheon of Rome. Notre-Dame Basilica (1824) resembles a medieval cathedral. The Old Seminary (1685), is Montreal's oldest building. Other structures ringing the plaza show a wide variety of architectural styles ranging from Art Deco, to Belle Epoque to Modern (1972).

Montreal History Center

Occupying the old fire station, the Montreal History Center, built in 1903, is an excellent place to visit to learn about the development of the city from the beginning of the last century till today. It is open Tuesday thru Sunday 10:00 to 5:00 and closed Mondays.

Granite Obelisk

Standing at the center of the Place d'Youville, the obelisk has the names of the original settlers etched into it. To the south is Governor Callière's mansion. Here the peace treaty between the Iroquois and French was signed in 1701

Notre-Dame Basilica

424 Rue Saint Sulpice
(514) 842-2925
http://www.basiliquenddm.org/en/

This is the heart, the focal point of Old Montreal. If your time is limited and you are unable to wander amid the old city, this is a must see. Originally built of wood inside the riverside fort guarding the city, today's structure was completed in 1829. Every December it hosts performances of Handel's 'Messiah.' In the summer the Montreal City Orchestra stages a Mozart festival. 11:00 A.M. mass each Sunday has a mixed choir singing in polyphony accompanied by the great organ. The interior has medieval walnut carvings, stained glass windows and 24 karat gold stars embedded in the ceiling.

Inside the cathedral is the Notre-Dame Museum. Here you will find a fine collection of embroideries, paintings, religious silver, and sculptures.

Parc du Mont-Royal

http://www.lemontroyal.qc.ca/en/learn-about-mount-royal/homepage.sn

Towering over the city is the 225 meter (739 foot) Mont Royal from which the city got its name. Named by Jacques Cartier in 1535, the 343 acre forested park hosts a variety of activities.

Here, in the heart of the world's great cities, can be found hundreds of varieties of birds as well as a host of other wild life. Designed by Fredrick Law Olmstead, the park is a favorite place for locals to spend the day jogging, hiking, bicycling, horseback riding or walking the dogs. In the wintertime you can cross-country ski or go sledding on the mountain side.

At the top of the mountains is Kondiaronk lookout. From here you get a spectacular 360 view of the city and its environs. Across from the lookout is the Chateau du Mont Royal. Concerts are staged here throughout the summer. Atop the mountain is the 40 meter (120 foot) Cross of Montreal. Illuminated at night, this cross commemorates city founder Maisonneuve who carried a cross up the mountain in 1643 as a way of giving thanks for sparing the city from flooding.

Olympic Park

4141 Rue Pierre De Coubertin
(514) 252-4141
http://www.tourisme-montreal.org/What-To-Do/Attractions/montreal-tower-olympic-park

Built for the 1976 Summer Olympics, Montreal's Olympic Park is as impressive as it is controversial. The imposing structure, costing over a billion dollars, was not completed until the 80's. Its retractable roof has never worked properly. Adjacent to the park is an enormous quadrilateral.

Here visitors can spend an afternoon looking at the sites and engaging in activities. Looming over the park is the largest inclined tower in the world. Riding the funicular to the top provides the best view of the city outside of Parc du Mont-Royal.

Near Olympic park is the **Biodome de Montreal.** A perfect outing for kids, the biodome is a former Olympic stadium that now houses four different ecological habitats- Marine, forest, rain forest and polar. Each is home to indigenous plants, animals and marine life. Group tours and individual tours are available.

La Ronde Amusement Park

22 Chemin Macdonald
(514) 397-2000
http://www.laronde.com/larondeen/

The largest amusement park in Quebec, La Ronde was constructed for the 1967 International and Universal Exposition (Expo 67). The park has forty thrilling rides and activities for people of all ages. Among the thrill rides are the Super Manège, Le Monstre, Cobra, Le Vampire, Goliath, and Vol Ultime. Among the many activities are the rock wall, slingshot and go karts. During the summer an international fireworks competition is held bi-weekly when people from around the world come to demonstrate the latest in fireworks.

Botanical Gardens

22 Chemin Macdonald
(514) 397-2000
http://espacepourlavie.ca/jardin-botanique

Considered one of the greatest botanical gardens in the world, the Montreal Botanical Gardens was designated a national historical site in 2008. This 190 acre park is home to over 26,000 varieties of flora. Ten greenhouses containing plants from around the world make up the greenhouse complex. The greenhouses are open year round while the grounds can be covered with snow from November to April. Spread out over the gardens, are a series of theme gardens.

Alpine Garden

Here you will find a wide variety of delicate flora and fauna usually found at high altitudes. These plants are found on a rocky outcrop ringed by several trails.

First Nation's Garden

The plants of Canada are found here. Among these are birch, maple and pine trees. Also found in this part of the garden are a variety of totem poles. Each pole is unique and depicts various styles of the native cultures.

Japanese Garden

Here you can stroll amid the bonsai trees and other traditional plants of Japan. In the garden is a Japanese style building which houses an exhibit on tea. During the summer a traditional Japanese tea ceremony takes place. Visitors can take classes to learn this venerable tradition. Other traditional ceremonies such as Laido and Ikebana take place in this building. On August 6th, a ceremony honoring the victims of Hiroshima takes place with an hourly ringing of the Japanese Peace Bell made in Hiroshima. The garden contains a large Koi pond. Occasionally visitors are allowed to feed the fish.

Chinese Garden

This is the largest Chinese garden outside of China. The garden follows designs from the Ming Dynasty (14th to 17th century). Strict adherence is paid to traditional styles of Chinese gardening. Paths meander through the garden and around an artificial mountain. A traditional Chinese style building containing penjing and bonsai is found here.

Additional gardens include a rose garden and a poison plant garden.

The garden is located on the north side of Plateau Mont-Royal in Parc Maisonnueve. During the summer the garden is open every day from 9:00 a.m. to 6:00 p.m. In the winter it is open Tuesday through Sunday 9:00 a.m. to 5:00 p.m.

St. Joseph's Oratory

3800 Queen Mary Road
http://www.saint-joseph.org/en_1001_index.php

Located on the west slope of Mont Royal, St. Joseph's Oratory is a Roman Catholic Church- the largest church in Canada and the highest point in Montreal. Construction began in 1904 on what was a small basilica. Over the years the church grew in size until it was completed in 1967. Built in an Italian Renaissance style, the church is topped by a copper dome that rises 100 meters (318 feet) into the air.

The dome is the third largest in the world behind the Basilica of Our Lady of Peace of Yamoussukro in Côte d'Ivoire and St. Peter's Basilica, Rome. The church is dedicated to St. Joseph, Jesus' earthly father and Canada's patron saint. Inside are found intricately carved murals and thousands of votive candles.

More than 2 million people visit the church every year. Devout Catholics will climb the church's 99 steps on their knees. St. Joseph's Oratory is open every day. Tours are available as long as mass is not in session. Admission is free though a donation is most welcome.

Montreal's Underground City

Montreal's underground city, with its 30 km (19 miles) of tunnels spread out over 12 square km (4.6 square mile) area, is the largest underground city in the world. Originally named RESO, homophone of the French word réseau or 'network', it was constructed for the 1967 World's Fair as a way of allowing tourists to enjoy what Montreal has to offer without having to brave the harsh winter. The city has more than 30 movie theaters, 200 restaurants, and 17,000 shops which is 30% of all the commercial space in Montreal. 80% of the business and residential space is found here. Among the many places found are apartments, condominiums, hotels, banks, museums, offices, universities and shops. One of the city's largest malls, Eton Centre is here as is the World Trade Centre and Bell Centre where the Montreal Canadians hockey team plays.

The city is accessed by more than 120 entrances spread throughout Montreal. It is home to 10 Metro stations and a bus terminal. Most parts of the city are open from 5 a.m. to 1 a.m. which are the same hours the Metro runs. Many entrances are open only during business hours. More than half-a-million people visit every day. Admission is free.

A map of the underground city can be found here: http://www.stm.info/english/info/souterrain2010.pdf

Jean Talon Market

This European market is the farmer's market of Montreal. Nearby farmers bring their food to be sold here. Vendors display everything from fruits, to vegetables, meat, fish and cheese. Open all year round, the market is thriving and bustling during the summer months. Whatever your tastes you can find it here from freshly cooked to raw food. While it is the perfect place to stock up on groceries, it makes an interesting walking tour as well.

Museum of Archeology & History

350 Palace Royale
(514) 872-9150
http://pacmusee.qc.ca/en/home

With its modern architecture, the Museum of Archeology and History is the perfect way to begin exploring old Montreal.

The museum houses an enormous collection of archeological and historical artifacts that provide a fascinating glimpse into the area surrounding Montreal before the settlers arrived.

Of particular interest is the underground part of the museum. Here you can view an archeological dig of the cities earliest settlement. Other exhibits give a background of the development of Montreal from its earliest days to the present. The museum is open Tuesday through Thursday 10:00 a.m. to 5:00 p.m. During the summer it is open on Mondays. Guided tours are available.

Museum of Fine Arts

1380 Sherbrook W.
http://www.mbam.qc.ca/

Considered to be Montreal's finest museum, the Montreal Museum of Fine Arts houses some extraordinary treasures. On permanent display are works by Rembrandt, Renoir, El Greco, Cézanne and Picasso. In addition to these international artists, the museum is home to some of the finest works by Canadian artists. Also on display are WWI artifacts, furniture by Frank Gehry and a collection of 18th century porcelain.

The museum is open Tuesday through Sunday mid-morning to 5:00 p.m. Admission to the regular exhibits is free. Special exhibits have an admission fee. Guided tours are available

Museum of Contemporary Arts

185 Sainte-Catherine St W
(514) 847-6226
http://www.macm.org/en/

This museum contains modern art from Canadian artists. Quebec artists are a particular specialty. It is the only place in Canada dedicated to contemporary art and contemporary performing art. Of the 15,000 works on display, 12,000 of the artists are still alive.

The museum contains paintings, sculptures, photographs, and videos.

Science Center

2 Rue de la Commune Ouest
(514) 496-4724
http://www.montrealsciencecentre.com/home.html

This museum is dedicated to science and technology. Lots of hands-on exhibits make this a fun outing for the whole family. The Museum also has an IMAX theater.

Quebec City

The oldest and only walled city north of Mexico is Quebec City. Quebec is an overlooked gem in North America. It is seldom mentioned as a vacation destination; you don't often, if ever, hear friends telling tales of having visited Quebec City. This is a pity as it is often considered one of the top travel destinations by leading travel magazines and guidebook companies. Quebec is unique in all of North America. First time visitors upon seeing the city are often struck by the old European look and feel. With its narrow, winding cobble stone streets, its 17th century architecture, and variety of shops, store fronts and restaurants, it is easy to think you are in an old town somewhere in France.

Enticing aromas fill the streets. Restaurants of all varieties can be found including those offering traditional Canadian food. The culinary highlights are its French restaurants and cafes. Walk down most any street in Quebec and you will be assaulted with the smell of fresh baked bread, buttery baked goods, delicious meals and fresh brewed coffee. But more than this, Quebec is a city of rich historical significance.

In 2008, Quebec celebrated its 400th anniversary and is a UNESCO World Heritage Site. Settled by Samuel de Champlain, in 1608 it quickly became the fortress capital of New France. The French controlled the city until 1759 when it lost it to the British during the Battle of the Plaines of Abraham. The French nobility fled allowing an influx of immigrants, especially Irish escaping the great potato famine, to flood the city. Despite this, city rulers allowed the inhabitants to retain their language and culture. The city remained in British hands until 1867 when the Dominion of Canada was formed.

English speaking tourists, especially those arriving by car, are often confounded by the lack of spoken or written English. Young people are often bi-lingual though this is not true throughout the city and its environs, as less than 1/3 of the population are bilingual. Often bilingual speakers will be found in tourist places such as hotels and restaurants, but places such as shops and boutiques can be a bit dodgy. Visitors arriving from upstate New York and Vermont where much of the writings in areas such as rest stops are bilingual, will be struck by the total absence of English the instant they cross the border.

This is found throughout the area where everything, be it road signs to grocery stores, is French. It is not uncommon to ask for assistance only to find the person speaks no English at all. Likewise, many of the signs and historical markers within the city are written in French. Lately an effort has been made to accommodate English speakers but visitors should be wary. While Quebec is part of Canada, the Quebecois are fiercely proud of their French heritage and cling tenaciously to it.

Getting There

Quebec City lies 250km (150 mi) to the northeast of Montreal. The drive from Montreal along highway 20 or 40 takes about three hours and is rather dull. Chemin du Roy (Highway 138) following the north bank of the St. Lawrence River is a bit more scenic. It is possible to make a long day trip but not recommended. Quebec will catch you unprepared for its beauty and history. At the least you should leave Montreal in the morning, spend the night and return late afternoon the following day.

A passenger train, the Quebec-Windsor, makes frequent arrivals at the port of Quebec, 450 Rue de la Gare du Palais. Along the way, this train will stop at Toronto and Montreal.

A bus station, Terminus Gare du Palais, 450 Rue de La Gare du Palais, handles frequent buses from Montreal.

Getting Around

The old town is surprisingly easy to see. Its short, winding streets make a walk around the old city very pleasant though care must be taken as many of the streets are made of uneven cobblestone. The city does have one steep, winding street, the Côte de la Montagne that connects the upper part of the city to the lower part and riverside. A tram or funiculaire connects the two parts of the city.

Tourists must take some care when crossing the street. You will notice that all traffic lights turn red while all the pedestrian lights turn white. This means that pedestrians can cross the street from both directions. When the traffic light is green and the pedestrian light is red, vehicles have the right-of-way.

Driving is possible but difficult for the newcomer. The streets are old and quite narrow. Many are one-way only and can easily catch an unwary driver off guard. Parking is difficult at best. Before driving into Quebec City, make sure you are aware of parking regulations and what to look for to insure you have found a legal place to park.

The city is crisscrossed by a public bus system. Tickets with transfers are good for unlimited travel in one direction for two hours. Pre-paid cards with 12 two-way rides are available from licensed vendors. You can also purchase tickets that a valid for 1, 2, 7 and 30 days.

When to Go

Quebec can be quite cold from November to March as temperatures hover at and below freezing. In the dead of winter, the St. Lawrence River freezes over. Late spring, summer and early autumn months can be quite pleasant as temperatures range from 41 to 56 °Celsius (56 to 74 °Fahrenheit).

What to See

Old Quebec or Vieux-Quebec. This is the part of the city designated a World Heritage Site by UNESCO. It is a walled city, the only one outside of Mexico. Beautiful shops and cafes line the cobblestoned streets. Old French style buildings with arched roofs to shed the snow invite gazing and picture taking. This part of the city contains the Citadel, Notre-Dame Basilica and Quartier Petit-Champlain. When the sun goes down the old city comes alive. Bathed in light and noisy from bars and music venues, it is reminiscent of the French Quarter in New Orleans. As you wander through the city, see if you can spot the cannon ball embedded in the roots of a tree.

The **Citadel** is the largest built British fortress in North America. Completed in 1850 the Citadel housed British troops and Regular Canadian Armed Forces. It has been in use ever since. Today it is home to the Royal 22e Régiment or the Francophone infantry contingent of the Regular Canadian Armed Forces. The Citadel is open every day depending on the season. Guided tours are available and recommended as it is a valuable source of information on the history of the region.

Next to the Citadel is **Battlefields Park**. This 267 acre park is often referred to as the Plains of Abraham. It was here the Battle of Quebec or the Battle of the Plains of Abraham took place on September 13th, 1759. It was battle during the French-Indian war that the French were forced to give Canada to the British.

The park itself is one of the great parks in North America. Strategically located, the park offers stunning views of Quebec and the St. Lawrence River. The Discovery Pavilion is a great place to learn more about the epic battles that took place on this spot. It is open 8:30 a.m. to 5:30 p.m. on weekdays and 9:00 a.m. to 5:00 p.m. on weekends.

Notre-Dame-de-Quebec Basilica is one of the oldest cathedrals in North America. It's easy to pass this basilica by as it does not have an inviting exterior. Don't be fooled. Its neo-baroque interior is one of exquisite beauty. The cathedral is gilded in gold leaf while colonial French art and decorations line the inside.

Terrasse Dufferin is a former military fortification. It now serves as a promenade running along the St. Lawrence River. It is a popular walk to view the old city, river and cruise ships that frequent the city. The walk takes you beneath the Chateau Frontenac, the most recognizable structure in Quebec. In the summertime, the Terrasse Dufferin is home to many street performers and artists. Guided tours are available from mid-May to mid-October.

TORONTO & MONTREAL TRAVEL GUIDE

Recommendations for the Budget Traveler

Places to Stay

Celebrities Hotel

1095 Rue Saint Denis South
(514) 849-9688
http://www.celebritieshotel-montreal.com/

The second most popular hotel in Montreal, the Celebrities Hotel is located in the Latin Quarter near downtown and Chinatown. Popular shopping stores and access to the underground city are within easy walking distance. With 26 rooms, travelers have four options to choose from: A family suite, a junior suite, a standard room with a private bathroom and a standard room with a shared bathroom.

A continental breakfast is included with some rooms. All rooms have a telephone, TV with satellite, and air-conditioning. Wi-Fi and high speed internet are available throughout the hotel. A continental breakfast is served every morning. The reception desk is open 24 hours a day. Prices range from $70 to $120.

Hotel de Paris Montreal

901 Sherbrooke East
(514) 522-6861
http://www.reservation-desk.com/hotel/239048/hotel-de-paris/photos/?TID=sOqeyUyQ5|pcrid|23880946077&utm_source=google&utm_medium=cpc&utm_term=hotel%20de%20paris%20montreal&utm_campaign=Hotel%20Chain%20H

This hotel is located in the plateau neighborhood. This swanky, upscale neighborhood has an energetic nightlife. This section of Montreal is popular with locals who frequent its many restaurants, cafes and bars. The hotel used to be a Victorian mansion. Its 34 rooms have either 1 double bed or 1 queen bed. Larger rooms come with 1 king or 2 queen beds. One room can hold 8 people. Each room comes with air-conditioning and a TV. Wi-Fi is available throughout the hotel and an internet workstation is available 24 hours a day. A continental breakfast is served every morning. With rooms between $80 and $140, the Hotel de Paris Montreal is ideal for both the budget and mid-range traveler.

Auberge Montreal Youth Hostel

901 Rue Sherbrooke E.
(514) 522-6124
http://www.aubergemontreal.com/

This reasonably priced hostel is located in the heart of Montreal. Its rooms hold between 4 to 14 people as well as private rooms with bathrooms. The hostel has PC's with internet access. Reception is open 24 hours and there is no curfew. Bunks are as low $23 and a private room is $80.

HI-Montreal Youth Hostel

1030 Rue Mackay
(514) 843-3317
http://www.hostellingmontreal.com/en/home.aspx?sortcode=2

Conveniently located between Concordia and McGill universities, HI-Montreal offers shared and private rooms. Wi-Fi is available. Its knowledgeable staff is a wealth of information for travelers. The hostel also sponsors pub crawls, bike tours and informative walks. If you'd like to catch a Montreal Canadiens hockey game the hostel sells tickets. Cost per night starts at $60.

Auberge De Jeunesse Alexandrie

1750 Rue Amherst
(514) 525-9420
http://alexandrie-montreal.com/?lang=en

The Alexandrie is not just a hostel. It also serves as a B&B and an apartment. Individual or groups of backpackers are welcome as are families. A kitchen and laundry is available as is free Wi-Fi and a phone for local calls. A continental breakfast is served every morning. Cost per room is about $60.

Places to Eat & Drink

Espace Cafe & Espresso Bar

210 Notre Dame West
(514) 284-8998
http://www.espacecafe.ca/

This family owned café is near Notre Dame. Renowned for its espresso and friendly staff, Espace cooks up a first-class meal at cheap prices. Its rankings are always among the highest of all Montreal's cafes. Meals are not pre-cooked but are prepared on the spot. The menu has an extensive list of sandwiches.

If you don't find what you want, they are more than happy to make you something to your specifications. Meals range from $5 to $10. Hours are Monday through Friday 8:00 a.m. to 5:00 p.m. and Saturday 9:00 a.m. to 5:00 p.m. The café is closed on Sunday.

Schwartz's

3895 Blvd St-Laurent
http://www.schwartzsdeli.com/

This popular café is a Hebrew deli. Popular with locals, some would call it legendary, Schwartz's is often quite crowded, and for good reason. Its smoked meats are cured on the premises without using chemicals, and are considered the best in Montreal. Favorites include brisket, turkey, chicken and duck. Its meat is served fat, medium or lean. Opening hours are Sunday through Thursday 8:00 a.m. to 12:30 a.m., Friday 8:00 a.m. to 1:30 a.m. and 8:00 a.m. to 2:30 a.m. Saturday. Prices range between $5 and $10.

La Banquise

994 Rue Rachel Est.
(514) 525-2415
http://labanquise.com/en/

Another eatery and brewpub located in the Le Plateau-de-Mont-Royal neighborhood. Popular with younger people, La Banquise is known for its traditional local dish called poutine.

Poutine is slightly similar to gravy and cheese fries. It has a flavor all its own that has to be tried. La Banquise serves over two-dozen varieties of poutine including a vegetarian one. It is well stocked with microbrews. La Banquise's kitchen is open 24 hours and prices range between $10 and $20.

Stash Café

200, Rue St.-Paul Ouest
(514) 845-6611
http://stashcafe.com/

Specializing in Polish cuisine, the Stash Café has the look and feel of old Montreal. Church pews are used as seats, wooden ceiling beams are exposed and the walls are made of ancient stone. Posters of musical and theatrical events are hung from the beams giving it a look of an Eastern Europe café. Among the menu favorites are potato pancakes, borscht, and pierogy. The Stash is open from 11:30 a.m. to 11:00 p.m. Dinners range from $15 to $40.

Vices et Versa

631 St. Laurent
(514) 272-2498
http://www.vicesetversa.com/

Considered by many to be the best beer bar in Montreal, Vices et Versa is more like a neighborhood pub than a typical bar.

If you've come to Montreal to sample the local beer, this is the place to do it. Vices et Versa is considered a mecca for beer lovers. The bar also has all manner of liquors.

A good menu is available for the hungry. Among the favorites are the pulled pork and poutine. Outdoor seating is available making it a convivial place to gather with friends or meet locals. It does not advertise itself well so you'll have to keep your eyes open or you'll walk right by it. Its hours are Tuesday through Saturday 3:00 p.m. to 3:00 a.m. and Monday and Sunday 3:00 p.m. to 1:00 a.m. Depending on what you drink and eat, a night at Vices et Versa will cost you between $10 and $50.

Places to Shop

Jeans, Jeans, Jeans

5575 Casgrain
(514) 279-3303
http://www.jeansjeansjeans.ca/

For those who complain that they can never find a decent pair of jeans that fit, your search is over when you stop in Jeans, Jeans, Jeans. Jeans are their specialty. It's what they do. Here you will find jeans of every size and every brand. With such a wide selection you are sure to find a pair of jeans that will fit your budget. The store features an onsite hemming service. Its hours are Monday through Wednesday 9:30 a.m. to 5:00 p.m., Thursday 9:30 a.m. to 9:00 p.m., Friday 9:30 a.m. to 6:00 p.m., Saturday 9:00 a.m. to 4:00 p.m., and it's closed on Sunday.

Harmonie Gifts & Souvenirs

1392 St. Catherine Ouest
(514) 399-9900

Not your typical gift shop. In addition to all the items you would find in a normal gift shop, Harmonie's also carries items that range from mildly expensive to very expensive.

If you're on a budget you will find a lot here; if money is of little concern, Harmonie's has what you're looking for. With such a large selection to choose from, you may find yourself walking out with items you would never have considered.

Mountain Equipment Co-Op

4394 Rue St. Denis
(514) 840-4440

Heated by geothermal energy, Montreal's Mountain Equipment Co-Op is a green store if ever there was one. This is the place to go if you are looking for outdoor gear and clothes. Backpackers needing to replace items of purchase things they forgot, find it to be an oasis. Whatever your outdoor needs you are sure to find it at the Mountain Equipment Co-Op. The Co-Op is open Monday through Wednesday 10:00 a.m. to 7:00 p.m., Thursday and Friday 10:00 a.m. to 9:00 p.m., Saturday 9:00 a.m. to 5:00 p.m., and Sunday 10:00 a.m. to 5:00 p.m.

Friperie Saint-Laurent

3976 Avenue Saint-Laurent
(514) 842-3898

If you're looking for vintage clothing from the 40's, 50's, 60's and 70's, this is the place to stop. Friperie Saint-Laurent has an astonishing variety of clothing that is nearly impossible to find elsewhere.

Not only are the clothes difficult to find, what they have is in nearly mint condition. If you're looking for that something special you remember from years ago, Friperie Saint-Laurent is worth a look. Its hours are Monday through Wednesday 11:00 a.m. to 6:00 p.m., Thursday and Friday 11:00 a.m. to 9:00 p.m., Saturday 11:00 a.m. to 5:00 p.m., and Sunday 12:00 p.m. to 5:00 p.m.

Chabanel Warehouses

This complex takes up eight blocks and is nine stories high. It is a bargain hunter's dream. If you can think of you, you most likely will find it at Chabanel Warehouses. Unlike most places in Montreal, you can haggle over prices to see if you can get a better deal. While some of the warehouses are open normal business hours, the main store is open Saturday's 9:00 a.m. to 1:00 p.m.

CPSIA information can be obtained
at www.ICGtesting.com
Printed in the USA
LVHW080904020423
743262LV00012B/584

9 781500 525958